The Sun Fetcher

Books by Michael Dennis Browne

The Wife of Winter (1970)
Sun Exercises (1976)
The Sun Fetcher (1978)

THE SUN FETCHER

poems by

Michael Dennis Browne

Carnegie-Mellon University Press
Pittsburgh & London 1978

Acknowledgments

Acknowledgment is made to editors of the following periodicals and anthologies in which these poems first appeared:

Ironwood, The American Review, Silo, The Seneca Review, John Berryman Studies, One, Minnesota Daily, Steelhead, A Lake Superior Journal, Green House, Aspen Anthology, A Review, Atlantic Monthly, Poetry Now, Dacotah Territory, The Lamp in the Spine, The New Yorker, Three Rivers Poetry Journal, Chicago Review, Antaeus, Crazy Horse, Studio One, The Nation, Hika Bay Review, The Iowa Review, Lillabulero, The Sensuous President (New Rivers Press), *Sound and Sense* (Harcourt, Brace, Jovanovich), *Best Poems of 1974* (Pacific Books), *A Tumult for John Berryman* (Dryad Press), *Twenty-Five Minnesota Poets* (#1 and #2) (Nodin Press), *The American Poetry Anthology* (Avon), *The Pushcart Prize* (Pushcart).

"Paranoia" first appeared in *Antaeus*. "In Switzerland" copyright © 1975, by The Atlantic Monthly Company, Boston, Mass. Reprinted with permission. "Morley, Winter, Maiden Rock" first appeared in *Chicago Review*, Vol 28, No. 4 1977, copyright © 1977 by *Chicago Review*. "Bird Before Dawn" first appeared in *The Nation*. "Fox," © 1974, The New Yorker Magazine, Inc.

"Fox" was awarded first prize in the Borestone Mountain Poetry Awards for 1974. It appeared originally in *The New Yorker* and then as a pamphlet printed by the Knife River Press.

"Sun Exercises" was originally published as a book by the Red Studio Press, with illustrations by Annie Hayes. I am grateful to Susan Winter for permission to reprint it here.

I would like to thank the Graduate School of the University of Minnesota for a grant in the summer of 1973 which enabled me to work on this book.

The rising of the sun
And the running of the deer,
The playing of the merry organ,
Sweet singing in the choir.

Traditional

for Paddy; the Pelican

CONTENTS

EPITHALAMION/WEDDING DAWN

for Nicholas & Elena

1

Happy the man who is thirsty.
And the moths, pilgrims to our screens.
The fisher stands waist-deep in the water,
waiting.   Happy the man waiting.

Who is not alone?   Who does not sleep
in the dark house of himself, without music?
The world, a collapsed fire, shows only its smoke,
and the smoke hides its hills,

hides, too, the places where we are sleeping,
the hand opened, the hand closed.
Fragments, the lovers lie.   And the question,
saying:

Who is broken?   No one is broken,
but the living are sleeping, like animals,
like the dead. Tree dreams
of the man he was, who walked

by the shore, who followed
the hill upward, who dragged his roots
through the universe, who lay down
to suffer there, and, loving the earth,

left it exhausted, returned to it renewed.
But the house is dark. The sky at such time
has no light.   Even the lines in the hand
are a little desert without name, and silent.

2

Friends; in the hours before dawn; the day of your wedding.
What will I tell you then?
That solitude's thorn
breaks into bloom now?   I think it is so.
I think that if we are scarred, light heals us now.
We can be heard, making our difficult music.
And for this the sun
drags itself up from the dark parts of the world,
again, again.
The windows take on the peculiar fire of the living.
The dog hoots like a wood-pigeon, he has *his* morning.

3

You must not be angry with this planet.
For we are in a company
whose music surpasses its pain.
For I tell you, I sat in the dark, also,
and the wedding light came onto my window,
and the hills were cleared for me,
and the field spread out in front of me, remarkable, like marble.
And I thought; this is their day,
how it breaks for them!
O sir, the angel flies, even with bruises
O lady, a bird can wash himself anywhere.
The dawn that came up the day of your wedding
took me in its hand like the creature I am;
and I heard the dark that I came from
whispering 'Be silent'.
And the dawn said 'Sing'.
And I found the best words I could find around me,
and came to your wedding.

THE DRIVING LESSON

I am teaching my brother to drive.

A swan is broken over the family.

Vast harsh movements of light over the land.   The winter
rolls her eyes, making belief.   We are small beneath the dry
dream of the sky.

Peter, great tears fall from the planet ahead of us.   I hold
my hand up, for I have seen the human thumb drown.

Now my brother makes his appeal in the Parliament of Snows.

How the snowfields shine in the dark!   And the farms are little
bright turrets of harvest.   We sing as we slide between such presences.

And now an animal breaks his paw at a keyhole.   A man shakes
to pieces in front of us.   There is something terribly criminal
around us.

We pass on the canal the swan and the snow-blind pilot.

And admit to being a target.   For the family begins as something you
drink from, clearly.   Then an abbey of black glass.   A hotel, veined.
The nose of the family bleeds.   Someone is on the roof.

Peter, though they break the swan.   Though we are spun out *un*lovingly.
The box of flares that rides the waves & will not burn.   The glass
of water on the branch.   With our feet firmly on the thunder.
Brotherhood, odd chariot, grand tour of the planets, brother good.

Hear it.   The soprano of wheat sings in space.   Insects in the same
ceiling.   *Dear God, time actually undresses us.*

Sitting down, moving.   Deciding, we turn here.   Queer red shine of the
ice, is it dawn, is it evening.   Some frigate, same flesh, some
journey. You listen to my ludicrous instructions. That, and my
other gift for you, this that you turn as you sit beside me,
this wheel, dear brother, this life that comes away in my hands.

15

HALLOWE'EN 1971

I carve my first head.   Then I carve another.
Now I have two Vietnamese
children on my table.

I place a candle in each of them, & light it.
The heads are still wet inside.   I've put
the seeds in a brown bag.

I take one head to the window.
The other I put on my stair, with the front
door open.   By it, a bowl of candy.

2

Down the block,
round the neighborhood,
all over this darkened country,
the hollow yellow heads
burning in windows, & tiny
American ghosts running toward them
through the dark, with open hands.

PEBBLE

I so loved the pebble
that now leaves my hand.
I do not throw it
& it does not fly from me.
Simply, it goes.

It is as if
it is washed smooth.
My kissing
did not do this,
time did it.
Before, I put my mouth
on a landscape.
Here is a plain now,
a slighter surface.
It hums off now
to its own future,
it is like a small moon
with a painted face
that leaves me.

I think if I opened
the door of my heart a little,
a little water would run out,
not blood.
It would flow after the stone,
following it.

OWL

to John Berryman

*On November 30th, 1972, a Great Horned Owl
was seen high in a tree on the University of
Minnesota campus, between Walter Library and
Johnston Hall. The owl stayed there all
day; by the following morning he was gone.*

He is there, with his large eyes,
high above us,
who were never close.
He will not say, he will not say
what it is he wants.
But we are glad he is there,
we without wings.
There is nothing he need not do.
And if he jumps,
we need not fear for him.

FALL JOURNAL, MAIDEN ROCK

October

I throw a clock on the fire
& my name over the edge.
Like an insect choosing to come
into a house in October,
I seek a yellow shadow.

October

A hundred wasps at the window.
A thousand insects still singing
in the grass in the garden.
Under the house the white stones
move; millions of them.

House, Fall

Flood of red light, & wind.
House of bricks; your ship will sink.
House of straw; your ship will fly.
Yes, my evening house, you are
red, a bird. The wind blows through you.
You are a dark bird.
You have eyes of fire.

Blood

There is blood, a ghost's blood.
It does not wash.
I wake covered
with grasshoppers, black leaves.
Butterflies,
with blood on their wings,
bring me an empty glass,
invite me to drink.

Wasps

The moon's striped children
creep together at night,
right by my bed, but the other
side of the window.
The frost finds them;
it turns their hearts, their wings,
to silver.

Pen

I have lost my new pen!
In a field an animal rises
with a pen in his hand.

Ships

A ship rocks back & forth
in the garage.
As I pull nails
from the ship in the living room
a new ship begins to form
in the garden.

November

A spider, with his few
belongings, laughing.
Moonlight.

SIX SPRING SONGS

1

My dog, and the moon,
know it is Spring;
once again they can see
their white faces in the water.

2

Working outside,
for 'dream' I type 'cream'.
I add an 's'
to a singular word, three times.
Three times I forget
to close a parenthesis.

3

dew drags
a child
over
grass

a bird
tastes
a twig

4

Someone sends me bread
through the mail.
Inside the loaf is a file.
I am not in jail . . .

5

for a moment
I hold together
the two pieces
of a broken bowl

6

The dog is asleep
on the floor, the cat is sleeping.
At the table a statue,
from whom ink is running.
In the dark, long before dawn,
a bird is singing.

THE PLANTS

1

In my house I keep green books,
whose pages turn without me.

2

You, window-friend, facing south,
you bear the dawn on your leaves
and the day's last blood.
And in that dawn how quickly
the dark's load slides from you.
And the mind more slowly
its bad dreams . . .
Jerusalem Cherry you are called.
And at Easter a tiny
green Christ rose up in your leaves.

3

You, darker friend, facing
your perfect twin in the mirror,
you, rooted but no prisoner,
you are small; but at night
I see myself sitting under you,
while the larger body is sleeping.
Australian Umbrella Tree.
With a wet cloth I wipe your leaves.
It is as if I clean a lens.
You go up into midnights.

4

And I want heart to be
a plant that in a dark house
stays wet, its leaves dripping;

a green book I keep,
whose pages turn without me.

CHILD OF MINNESOTA

In a rowboat in a green field
I see myself sitting.
The boat half-eaten,
the boat with the mark of many mouths on it.
A tornado passes, but this time silently,
with a child in its center, turning.

As the child is torn apart above me,
like a dandelion by the fingers,
I offer up my riddled boat in his name.
I vow to row the rest of my life in that field,
gathering his limbs as they descend,
year after year, out of the air.

ON THE ARREST & DEPORTATION OF SOLZHENITSYN

1

If there is a knock at the door
    it will be someone to check the furnace.
If there is a knock at the door
    it will be a collector for the Heart Fund.
If there is a knock at the door
    it will be a man with a pizza.

2

And the wife & child of Miguel Hernandez
lived on bread & onions,
while the poet went on down to his death in prison,
while the poet sat in the dark
with his eyes open
& wrote of moon & breast & the bird
that bursts up out of the mortal clay;
& instructed his tiny son
to laugh, *often.*

3

Here in this small Wisconsin town,
on winter Saturday nights
snowmobiles rack the lake & valley.
The two taverns are full.
The snowfields shine, the night
is thick with stars!
And the white dog wants to come
up on the bed by me,
while I read Hernandez; I let him.

4

If there is a knock at the door
     it will be seven men in snowmobile suits.
If there is a knock at the door
     it will be a child & a woman standing in the snow;
     an odor of onions.
If there is a knock at the door
     it will be a man who wants to use the phone;
     he asks the operator for Moscow.

*Miguel Hernandez, a Spanish poet, was imprisoned by Franco
and died in a Spanish prison in 1942, at the age of 31.*

IN SWITZERLAND

Solzhenitsyn puts on his glasses.
He has flowers in his hand.
He runs toward the plane, jumps up the steps
like a young man.

A camera in the plane pushes up close
to show the man and wife
hugging and embracing in the plane,
many small quick kisses.

The reporter says; still, it is a bit flat.
Leaving her homeland was obviously bitter for her.
They embrace, they embrace in Switzerland,
which gave them visas.

We see them driving off in a dark car,
one small son seated on the father's knee,
a hand stroking and stroking his head.
For hours the hand travels over

the valleys and villages, the rivers and forests,
the hills and wheat-fields of the child's head.

CRAB

. . . eyes on stalks!

When he sees me, stops.
I stop too.

Then a movement, sideways,
bulky, blueish, a tank,
but mincing almost,
picking at the path,

one large claw held
on his left side.

Such a square head!
But the ends
of what he walks on,
armored higher up,
low down are soft,
fine, like feelers.

Such mixtures
of soft spikes & solids,
this crab!

If the moon had creatures . . .
& he is a bit of a moon,
mauve rock-lump with moon-claws,
blueish deluxe walker,
going sideways.

Then, when he's
nearer the grass,
skips suddenly,
making me jump,
fizz of the little moon-piece
sideways from me
into the grass.

Clearly he feels safer there.

And watches;
palms turning over me,
sun burning us both;
moves off from me.

And men walk into the sea.

Tobago

CHICKADEE

Chickadee—
don't be afraid of me.
I am the one who feeds you.
Chick-chick-chickadee!

Here I am, come here!
A scarecrow with fat hands
of corn & sunflower seeds.
Come & feed from me.

Let all birds come, all kinds;
I can buy, I can buy
good seeds for you
all winter long, O tiny tribes!

Friends of the air,
don't be afraid of
the coming cold.   Like a magic man
in the fall I'll put out

cornseed, and at solstice
sunflower, flowers of the sun.
Chick-chick-chickadee!
You can rely on me.

CAPTAIN CAT

My cat has no desires.
He could sleep for a hundred years.
Captain Cat.   Captain Castrati.

He climbs a tree & thinks
he's an owl.   He is, he is.
He floats to my hand,
there is a candle in his claw.

My cat has no desires.
Aloft in the garbage he strums
the harp of the dead fish.
He is not in the snow,
he is in Mexico.

Captain, when you wake
in a hundred years,
stretch, yawn,
do all the things that you do.
We will be here, the dog & I,
by the fire.
It is only snow coming down
through the open roof.
And soon we will fix you some supper.

WHALE MUSIC

1

The whales are over London.
I am born under the stairs.
Children take off their clothes on the moon.
Surgeons hurrying toward them on the moon.
Smoke signals from the moon.
A map is in prison.

2

Children, eat your food,
the whales are coming.

I see no end to their cry.
A circle of light & mist that goes
round & round each country.

Our tiny boats bump on the surface.

The whales live in old buildings,
brick by wet brick they re-build them.

I hear, if I listen hard, their city.

3

As if I rode a door down.

I said to the door, *down;*
& it took me down.

There was no house on land I wanted,
& I wanted a place out of the wind.

Tired, scared, like a snail.
Full of fear.

I went down.
Out of my music, out of yours.

Not because I was bored but because
it was about time.

4

Like a soft root in the dark.
A little package of distress.

The wooden horse in the nursery.
I am inside, waiting.

The whales brush by the window.
The carol-singers with lanterns hurry past

the black & fishy bushes.
The whales are coming up the stairs.

I fear the fish,
& I fear the death of the fish,

whose death wets me.

5

The tree snaps open,
the black dog breaks out.

Beware the black dog.

Whose bite makes men mad,
even where they lie
deep in their farms.

Look out your window—a moon
falls, & shatters in a field.
Look out your window—a black dog
runs in the field, eating
all he wants.

The black dog,
biting open a moon.

The furniture moves around in the dark,
bumping, soft curses.
Even the chairs you sit on
want a piece of the light
to pin to themselves.
Even the sofa wants to share
in the death of the moon.

Keep the doors closed.
Black dog.   Black farms.

6

My father has no shadow,
& I stand in it.

O long, long
in the belly of the father.

The child sits on the piano-stool,
crouches, goes *into* the stool
& is not seen.

Is there music without him? *You* tell me.

What you take up to love
you will lose by evening.

To go home, to enter
the house.

To float, to do
the dark swim at dusk.

You,
lighting no lamps.

7

The map in my hand goes wet.

Spray from the end of the nineteenth century
flies in my face
as my father is born.

I am standing on the shore
watching him come out of the water.

Now, go to the library, to borrow your father.
Now, poke his grave, to keep it warm.

As if a man bandaged himself,
the bandages go wet
with the sweat of childhood.
His skin is awash.

Wet stars.   Wet planets.
A whole tree is soaked.

A man runs through the streets in alarm,
he is wet.

Pieces of the map lie on his shoulders,
pieces of the moon stick to his fingers.

He goes berserk in the neighborhood,
he feels he is so wet.

Do you not see how wet I am?

Or he lies on his back
in his father's belly

as at dusk the house
cuts loose & floats,

the fish move between stars,
between moons that move on the water.

The sun casts his hooks for him
but they dangle above him.

Easy to lie,
soft, a tulip, unborn,
folded over,
a two-month foal.

This is the dark farm,
this is the belly.
This is the whale of dead music,
this is the father.

The stars
float, the fish
slip in & out of the stars.

Sun, you fisher of men,
come, cut me out.

WAYS OF LOOKING AT SNOW DOG
for Keith Gunderson

1

In sleep, there is nothing I cannot do,
& I love my extraordinary life.

But in the sun through the window
I see the human hand lift into light,

& my dog's dish is empty.
And I rise, as all the world rises,

going for water.

2

He sighs.
When I am making
a point about poetry in class,
he lets out
such a sigh, *I've heard it*
all before, dear
but repetitive master.

When I am reading out loud
& reach a part of a poem
I care about,
he will rise, & start
to chase his tail.
I lose my listeners.

He climbs all over my students.
He will chase anything
to lick it.
There is just about nothing
he will not kiss.
Especially small children;
he sprints after them
while the mothers stand
paralyzed;
and he slobbers all over them.

3

you are the magic dog, at night a lost sailor looks out of
       your eyes
you are the magic dog, so white, when I take you skiing
       they say, *see, he talks to himself*
you are the magic dog, you chase squirrels, you will never make it
you are the magic dog, at night you float, you bear
       the children on your back
you are the magic dog, you growl in the house, you bark
       at the footfall
you are the magic dog, when I get sad & sunk in my life,
       there is your life in front of me, shaming my sadness
you are the magic dog, at the parking lot the attendant sees
       you in the back & asks if I will park the car myself,
       I explain your kindness
you are the magic dog, you peed on the office Christmas
       tree, well, you must think, inside or out, a tree
       is a tree is a tree is a tree

4

Sometimes I think he is wise.
He is a guide, a little mythical.

Sometimes he gives me long looks,
he has grave eyes.

Sometimes he has the face of my father.
But when I call him, he comes,
as the dead man does not.

Sometimes when he lies half-sleeping on the floor
I say his name, or praise him,
& his tail breaks the silence,
thump, thump, thump.

Sometimes he lays his jaw on my shoe
& I feel far below us
another pair is there,
the skull of a head
on the skull of a foot, resting.

5

The stick!   The stick!
You want the stick,
any stick will do,
the stick is sweet to you!

It flies through the air
like a bone filled with fuel,
you wrench it off the earth
& bring it right back.

But you don't *give* it back.
You run circles around me, the best game.
All over the planet, in parks,
breathless men pleading with their dogs

for the magic wand in their jaws.

6

In the dark wind I run with my dog.

He is so white, he is like snow,
& I call him so.
I take the garbage out in brown bags
& I put a match to it.
The flames jump up,
the flames of human rubbish
light up his eyes.

7

At night I lie
stretched out, still.
I am the knight on the tomb, marble,
and you are the hound
carved forever at my feet.
But we breathe.

8

At the clinic he goes in
the entrance for SMALL ANIMALS.
A small horse.   Eighty pounds.
They run a test on his eyes
& the rims go green.
Then the green runs out of his nose.
He sits, wretched
on the metal table
with his white-and-green clown face.
His eyes are fine.
For years he can go on running
ahead, taking me deeper.

9

At the zoo too he is small.
When I feel he's getting superior,
bigger than most
dogs on the block,

I take him to the lion, the Bengal tiger.
He can't quite believe what he sees.
He shrinks back;
why have you brought me here?

The white she-wolf, when she sees him,
moans & whines,
she wants to be with him.
But the cougars in the next cage

tear up & down, they fly against the bars,
they want to rip him apart.
I take him off, to chase a safe stick in the park.
There are enough claws around us.

10

He sheds.
I have never seen anything like it.
He carefully chooses
the place to shake himself,
a rug just swept,
a floor just cleaned.
He walks about the house
spraying his white hairs.
When he sleeps on my bed
I wake up old.

11

He likes best to chew
the human hand.
For him it's a kind, inexhaustible object,
a sort of soft sculpture
he can get his teeth into.

And he bites on
my fear of living. When I feel
such life on the end of my hand,
tugging me out of my dark,
he seems to be saying—

O man too used to the moon,
leave your dark farm
where the tears fall thick,
I'll lick them off with my tongue.

He seems to crow—

Cock-a-doodle-beginning,
cock-a-doodle-beginning,
rise, rise,
leave your bad bed.

Each stick thrown
is one move forward.
Each walk undertaken
is one shadow not stayed in.

12

I saw the dog's dream

he smelled the summer on the window
he danced with stiff hips

I saw the dog's dream

in the storm he dreamed of his son
the dog wrapped a harp in a blanket

I saw the dog's dream

he sucked a light-bulb as it burned
he ran to the pool where the neighborhood dogs swam weeping

I saw the dog's dream

the bone came down in the form of a cloud
the white boat slipped from her mooring

two by two the white dogs go
over the glass harbor

13

you are the magic dog, sweet hound, we will not meet in Heaven
you are the magic dog, utterly useless as a telephone answering
        service

you are the magic dog, when the car radio played 'Jingle Bells'
    performed by a chorus of singing dogs you nearly
    fell off the seat
you are the magic dog, when you eat your red meat I am far from
    you
you are the magic dog, when your nose is deep in another dog,
    you hardly hear me
you are the magic dog, I will never own you
you are the magic dog, you will never see Denmark
you are the magic dog, your white bark flies up to be the moon
you are the magic dog, you sing to the prisoners
you are the magic dog, you scratch at the screen
you are the magic dog, & you want to come in

well, well, come in then, welcome

FOX

Driving fast down the country roads.
To a committee.   A class.
When I stop for gas, a highway patrolman tells me
one of my lights is out.
Then he drives off to take up his position
behind a bush at the bottom of the hill
to wait for speeders.

Yesterday, a snake, black & green, coiled
down by the railroad tracks.
His mouth bloody, he moved slowly,
he looked like he was dying.
Boats being pulled up out of the water.
The dog ran into the lake
after the sticks the children threw,
and stood looking back at me from the gold water.

On TV, the faces of the captured Israeli pilots.
Syrian film of Israeli planes crashing,
martial music.   The patrolman crouched behind the bush,
the mouth of the snake, hard & red,
his green-black body without ease,
a bent stick by him, as if maybe
a child had beaten him with it, maybe the same
child throwing sticks to the dog in the water.

Hurrying through Wisconsin.
Hundreds of black birds tossed up
from a cornfield, turning away.   Arab or Israeli?
The man in the parked patrol car,
the sticks rushing, failing through the air.
County Road Q, Country Road E.
The committee meeting, waiting for me.

The fox! It is a fox! It is a red fox!
I slow up. He is in the road.
I slow. He moves into the grass, but not far.
He doesn't seem that afraid.
Look, look! I say to the white dog behind me.
Look, Snow Dog, a fox! He doesn't see him.
And this fox. What he does now is
go a little further, & turn, & look at me.
I am braked, with the engine running, looking at him.

I say to him, Fox—you Israeli or Arab?
You are red; whose color is that?
Was it you brought blood
to the mouth of the snake? The patrolman
is waiting, the dog standing
in the gold water. Would you
run fetch, what would you
say to my students? He looks at me.

And I say, So go off, leave us, over
the edge of that hill, where we shan't see you.
Go on—as the white she-wolf can't,
who goes up & down, up & down
against her bars all day,
all night maybe.

Be fox for all of us, those in zoos,
in classrooms, those on committees,
neither Assistant Fox nor Associate Fox
but Full Fox, fox with tenure, runner
on any land, owner of nothing, anywhere,
fox beyond all farmers,
fox neither Israeli nor Arab,
fox the color of the fall & the hill.

And you, O fellow with my face,
do this for me; one day
come back to me, to my door,
show me my own crueller face, my face
as it really cruelly is, beyond what

a committee brings out in me, or the woman
I love when I have to leave her.
But no human hand, fox untouched, fox
among the apples & barns, O call out
in your own fox-voice through the air over Wisconsin
that is full of the falling
Arab & Israeli leaves, red, red,
locked together, falling, in spirals, burning . . .

be a realler, cleaner thing,
no snake with a broken body, no bent stick,
no patrolman crouched behind a bush
with bloody mouth, no stick thrown,
no beloved tamed dog in the water . . .

And let us pull up now out of the water
the boats, & call the leaves home
down out of the air, Arab or Israeli;
& you, my real red fox in Wisconsin,
as I let out the clutch & leave you,
you come back that time, be cruel then,
teach me your fox-stink even, more than now, as I
hurry, kind & fragrant, into committee,
& the leaves falling, red, red.
And the fox runs on.

MAD BOOK, SHADOW BOOK
Further Stories of Mr. Michael Morley

"Blessed be the Lord, for He has wondrously shown
His steadfast love to me when I was beset in a
besieged city."

*

Michael Morley creaked through the midnight wood
like a grandfather clock.
All the shadows followed
as if he were raw meat.
He slid over the snow
like a skillet down a slope, he was electric!
Morley broke into an empty classroom
& took off his wheels.
He broke into a ladder full of photographs,
he set up a photograph of a ladder
against a waterfall.
He ran up the waterfall
& set the fish on fire!

*

GRIM SONG OF A SORT

I try to lift up
what I bury,
but I bury it.
The burning bush, buried.
The swimming woman, buried.
I rowed toward the heart,
but it sank.
I buried the boat.
I tried to lift
the ship but I buried it.
The dog found the ship
& sails it now.
I tried to lift
the sitting position

49

but it fell down
to be buried, knew
it would be buried.
I found
the faults of the earth
& buried things there.

I stared
at the sun-burying sea
& I buried the sight.
All in a day's
work. Night comes.
I bury my head, I go home.

*

BICYCLING

I want to go bicycling
with my friends
the Russian poets!
I would kiss the red dust
of that air, really!
I want to go into
a wood temple, in the
yellow pasture.
Oil on my ankles,
oil along my veins.

*

MORLEY MINNEAPOLIS DARK JOY

In silence a Morley spreads his wings.
By firelight he flies round a room.

Full professors lie on their backs
& stare at the stars.
A child is crushing mushrooms.

He sees the house in the desert,
the diver riding the octopus
through the desert,

he sees an Alp on its side,
the snapped bridge mending,
the ballroom, rising, lifted by moons.

She lifts her legs higher,
he shines like a ghost town.
A child pauses, to forget something.

Now a moon is in front of her,
its pages whirling.

*

OCTOBER

The quality of it
goes, like a violin

into space.   Spaces
of October, morning.

A bird rises
from out of an iron bar.   Gold
comes out of our mouths.

*

ACORNS, OCTOBER

And so, falling.
And so, a pool that holds

onto a doorknob,
a hanger of dazzling, the

roof, pop.   There's no
end to this, the dark

roof growing wider, the
falling.   Lie there,

listening.   And so, in the
world, on the planet.

*

"GENTLE"

If anyone uses
the word "gentle" once more
in a contemporary American poem
I'm going to fix him/her
to the wall of a crypt
wth a power drill.

*

INSPIRATION POINT
(after Apollinaire)

They think I am sitting alone at the front of the boat
because I want to be inspired.
"Is that Inspiration Point?" somebody asks.
I don't want to be inspired,
I want to look at the water.

*

MORLEY, WINTER, MAIDEN ROCK

1

I feel good running
so I run & run.
I run through the wood in a hood.
I run through a pie
my mother is making in England.
I run through my brother's fingers
as he lifts his hand to his head.

52

And I dump & burn my winter hands.
I burn the Winter Man.
I snap Death's stream on my knee.
I am the King who had been hiding
in the tree.
I run through the ruins,
restoring the ruins as I run.

2

I go out early to see the dog
practicing trying
to write his name in the snow.

Or, when no one sees him, the dog
climbs the hill behind the house
& digs for a bone he has buried.
Jog, jog, back to the front of the house
with it in his jaw;
& sits & chews on it.
No one has taught him to do this!

Meanwhile the cat
swings from a dead tree
until it is green.

3

FALLING ASLEEP IN THE AFTERNOON

Again I am
falling asleep in the afternoon;
not "falling in love again" but
falling asleep in the afternoon.
The glass in the window thickens
until only the room is mine.
And then the room inside the room,
through which I begin to run.

COMPLINE (Being the Monastic Night Prayer)

Frogs, sing your Compline,
          Our Lady of Pads,
          Our Lady of Radar,
Pond-Monks,
   cash register on the moon,
          Our Lady of Pond,
          Our Lady of Packages,
Frogs, come to the Lord,
Frogs, fear not the terrors of the night,
     "nor the planes come in",
          Our Lady of Protein,
          Our Lady of Prose Fiction,
Frogs,
      Salve Regina,
      Hail Holy Vitamin,
make ready the body.

Amen, Amen,
a good night to us all, no phone calls,
          Lady of Pad,
          Lady of Pond.
     Laundry
         Amen.   Amen.

*

EARTH DAY

Books go by on the wind.
Dance, distance, & beasts.

I see flames, a city,
maybe. Dancing.
Books; on the wind.

My lover, why do you slither
down the tree? To place
on your plate
the steak of melody.
And you shall be sheriff too.

Thank you, thank you.

*

THE ATOMIC THUMB

The Morley sat in a trench on the Eastern Front
absolutely browned off with Hitler.
A woman slept up.
When Hitler smiled The Morley's
buttons booed.
When Hitler smiled, horses knew.
The Morley sat in the trench's stench.
When Hitler smiled a toad
rolled out of his record collection.
A woman sat up & slept.

*

MAGI

When the frankincense
hits the fan, the three
wise men strap on their skis
& drift toward Jesus.

*

DIALOGUE

Hallo, birds.
                    Good afternoon, sir.
Food OK?
                    Yes thanks, Morley. Morley, are you a
                                        little better?
Yes thanks, birds. Birds . . .
                    Yes?
You are welcome here, plenty of you, on the planet, balcony,
feeding, the little red seed house, you . . .
                    Stop, stop, we are embarassed!
Chickadees, may you never twitch your wings in shadow.
                    Thank you, sir. Thank you. Thanks. Exactly.

*

MORLEY & ULLA
(Tobago)

The leaf shines.
However dark the tree

the leaf must shine.
As the mind, loved.

The leaf under the sun,
that cannot keep from shining.

*

THE FEAST OF THE IMMACULATE CONCEPTION
(December 8, 1972, Dinkytown)

A raft heaped with padlocks drifts down 4th St.
I nail the Edict of Nantes to the door
of an Italian restaurant.
I rush through the health food store
spreading news of the Immaculate Conception.

56

A policeman in a blue veil
is floating toward me over the roofs.
I put a gun to my mouth,
or maybe it is a bagel.
Yep, I would rather
eat than shoot.

*

SEVEN AGES

A Morley hurries through the streets,
carrying a target, whose colors run.

A worried-looking Morley with my face
runs to a grave, points, & shouts
"The enemy is *there!*"

A Morley sits in a closet & screams
"Women are walking by my grave!"

Eyes closed, a Morley speeds round
a house. Children come into the house,
huge fragments of aircraft in their hands.

A Morley struggles to tug
an arm from a grave.

A Morley sits at a tiny desk on the moon,
an arrow in his back.

A Morley, a man-child, falls
in flames from a piano stool.

*

DIAMOND

I rode the horse of winter
till it cracked beneath me
like a chandelier.

Inside me is a sea.
Part of the sea is on fire.

*

If a log rings in the fire—
don't answer it!

*

ANOTHER EVENING

Parking too close to another car, I get out
as if I have been shot.
I try to open the door of my house
with the key to the trunk of my car.
In the kitchen I open a can of soup & jump in,
closing the lid over me.

*

RICE SONG

From the cold typewriter,
smoke!
The rice is on fire!
The rice we threw at the poem,
the air force of rice!
(The dog sucks a plum,
the cat blooms.)
The rice scattered in the dark & dingly dell,
the mad late rice of Henry Purcell!

*

A Morley cries
at the flames on his arms.
A Morley carries a window through a wood.
A Morley is invited, he does not attend.
A Morley is damaged, he does not mend.
In sleep I lie on a door
& the door opens & I go there.

NOVEMBER

The tree shakes.
I shake myself.
This is what we do.

The fly, his frenzy.
Likewise, I know it.

Early, earlier, I turn
on the lamp.
This is what we do.

*

WIND, SEPTEMBER

Shadow.   I mean shadow.
Blood through the body.

I mean the hill burning inside.
I mean the hair is loose, only.

House in shadow, dog.
Suddenly bright, better.

I mean a wind for all of us.
I mean the hill behind.

*

I was with people who looked up to see
birds flying south, above the woods.
'Canadian geese', flying 'South', 'together',
in 'October'.
And these are our woods where we are walking.
And we are together on the ground.

*

A Morley leaps through
the hole his wit has made
in an opponent.
I have been waiting for you, says the spider.

*

Here is a storm
to place in your pie
said the bird, the thunder bird.

I can go no further, said the door-knob.
I'm glued to the moon, an owl said.
O my dears, we are all upside down
said the room, said the wrong room.

Calm down!
shrieked a worm.

*

The moon lights the snow.
I see my house from a distance.

My steps snap the snow-crust.
The dog treads on top, ghostly.

I look back to see my upstairs window.
The light is on.

This is where we sleep,
this is where we live, under the sky.

The moon shines,
the greater window.

*

SPIDER

The spider churns
his disc of light,

the leaf
bakes a medal.

You go to grab,
forest grabs *you*,

now you're one
of its spiders,

a little baker,
8 legs, all busy.

*

SEPTEMBER 1973

A hill.   Down which
a clarinet slides.

I am a serpent in the grass.
I want to sleep forever with my love.

The wind blows
over the dead, not through them.

O,
stars.

In the hallway is
a child.

He raises his tiny fists
& punches huge holes in me.

*

CHRISTMAS 1972

I have two presents;
a book, & a small wood box.
The book is mightier than the box.
Let us keep things that way.

*

SLEEP

Sleeping anywhere in the house.
Sleeping a lot, like a dog.
Stretch out.

You can sleep on the floor.
Over in a corner.
Sleep on a table,
coiled round the sewing machine.
Sleep wherever you like,
because this is your house.

You can dream of a woman;
probably you do.
Men dream of women, oh yes they do!

Minnesota; sounds of the sea.
The fog floats in, anywhere.
Three times a minute
your bed gives off the ancient cry
in case there are other beds in the room,
unseen, adrift like you.

Drift, drift.
Water all round the house
and in the house.
And where is the edge of the world?
Other sleepers, other beds.
You are never alone.

*

LATE SUMMER STORM

And the man bursts out of the house
in the canoe of the first passion,
his paddles flash as he
flows out of the flower,
as a wolf in his sweat
& power of paddles,
riding out, out!
Canoe of brash petals!
What weird tide you ride,
your white crown running,
wild under your fat crown of flowers!

*

THE SLEEPERS

The sleepers. I would like to bring them
bread when they wake, a red
handful of the dawn I pulled down, sheaf
of the gold trees in the street,
O shadow of the black horse I saw,
I would lift off the roof of the low house
& bring these gifts in,
like a key come home,
& lay them, like fruit, in festival,
among the leaves & branches of the sleepers.

*

The dog shakes that old shoe
the dawn in his young jaw
till the sky is in shreds.

The cat jumps on the dog's back
& raps his skull with a spoon
& rides him all the way home!

*

POEM WITH REPEATED PHRASE

The child asleep in the glass
The child asleep in the desk
The child asleep in the body
The child asleep in the amnesty
Red cross

The homework asleep in the body
The breast asleep in the academy
The dog asleep in the planes
The birth asleep in the cruiser
A cushion called Canada

The child asleep in the argument
The child asleep in the circles
The child asleep in the oil
The oil asleep in the South

'strangely weak aircraft'

*

I push my nose deep into her hair.
There is a smell of burning.
Yes, her head is on fire . . .
I will not put it out!

*

How strange to be on the earth,
and leave it only in sleep.
We are like tobacco coming back
into the cigarette . . .

*

THE KING OF CIRCLES

The King of Circles
hides in the grass near the house.
The King of Circles
flies over the house,
circling, calling,
"Who are you, are you?"

I am the Prince of Pieces.
I am here, I hear you.
I am filling my house
with a leaf from each tree.
From them I will make one leaf
by which men shall know me.

*

THE MAN

A man comes in the door
who makes your skin shiver.
He says: *I want the television.*
You say: *Have it.*
He says: *I want the dog.*
The dog, you say, *is more difficult.*

You wrestle; he is a snake,
he is fast, he is all over you,
his nails rip your back.
Darling, you say.
He tears the stocking from his head
& is the girl of your dreams.

*

Vermont, Minnesota

THINGS DROPPED

I wake up against the wall shouting "Don't drop it!"
as Jenny overloads a paper plate with food.
These past two weeks, the things we've dropped . . .
Apricot brandy on the carpet,
candle wax on the lace tablecloth,
cherry phosphate on your legs at the lunch counter,
Jason, the doll, in the woods, irretrievable,
your contact lens in the grass,
marshmallows into the fire, slices of hamburger.
Carla dropped a full book of tickets at the carnival,
Jenny a can of Alpo all over the kitchen;
and socks, napkins, soy sauce, blood, bits of lettuce . . .
I am amazed gulls do not follow
screeching in our wake,
such debris these lovers leave!
The only thing I have not dropped is your heart,
which I hold, and will not let fall.

PARANOIA

When you drive on the freeway, cars follow you.

Someone opens your mail, two hands
that come out of your shirt-sleeves.

Your dog looks at you, he does not like you.

At the driving test the cop is tired. He has sat up
all night, screening your dreams.

If you go to the zoo, be sure to take your passport.

Everywhere you go, the dog goes with you. Beautiful women
come up to you and ask for the dog's telephone number.

You go to teach; everyone who passes you in the corridor
knows you never finished *Tristram Shandy*.
You are the assistant professor no one associates with.

At the yoga class you finally get
into the lotus position.
You are carried home.

When you close your eyes in meditation, all you see is breasts.

When you turn the refrigerator to de-frost, the TV drips.

Across the street, the pigeons call softly to each other
like the FBI on a stakeout.

When you walk to the post office and see the flag at half-mast
you know you have died.

ROBERT BLY GETS UP EARLY

At the ticket counter, Minneapolis Airport, 7:30 am, standing in
line—a hand on my shoulder! It is Robert Bly! Risen like a
silo from out of the dark earth for one last greeting.

He is flying to Boston to read.   Flying to Boston with a satchel
of red bees.   "I have red bees in my bag.   I will have no
hesitation in releasing them into your unconscious."

Robert Bly!   Organic Foods!   White Poncho!   Vitamin E!

I get on my plane, sit down with Esquire, the New Yorker, and Greek
Lyric Poetry.   I reach for my notebook to write down a few bad
lines about Robert Bly unexpectedly putting his hand on my shoulder
so early in the morning at the airport—when a man sits down beside
me—it is Robert Bly!

This plane goes to Pittsburgh but he has charmed his way harshly
past the stewardesses.   He flies simultaneously to so many places
in his head, why should he not think that the Pittsburgh plane will
take him also to his reading in Boston—perhaps even directly to
the podium!

What does this manic Son of Norway want of me?   He shoves a small
blue book into my hands.   It is by a young Norwegian poet who is
traveling around the country in a Greyhound Bus with his girlfriend.

Do we have money for him, he asks?   His eyes crackle with the lustre
of Vitamin E.

O Robert Bly, you are on this earth only briefly, like an angel
with a hangover.   I see you striding, wings folded, across the
main lobby of the Minneapolis International Airport, pushing a vast
plow.   From the shattered floor foams a tide of soldier ants,
Latvian attorneys, centurions, phantoms, admirals, minor poets with

half-opened parachutes. They flow out of the airport and into the landscape, determined to turn the country around.

O Robert Bly, get off my plane! I have two readings of my own to do in Pittsburgh!

Robert Bly hurtles to gate 7a with his satchel of bees. He gets on his plane—at last! He needs no charm now—he has a ticket! From deep in the poncho he releases a bee. The bee makes his way forward into the cabin, crawls up onto the pilot's shoulder, and croaks into his ear: "Take this plane to 4th-century Tibet."

BAD POEMS

Bad poems are lying around
in huge jugs; I will not drink them!
I take a piece of beer
& nail it to the sky.
Driving, I see a nun crossing the road
& step on the gas-pedal, & get her;
these bad poems will disguise themselves
as anything!
I wake one morning
with cobwebs between my thighs;
I rush to the bathroom—
the dentures of hundreds of bad poems
piled in the bath-tub.
That night, when I switch on
my lamps, bad poem moths
storm them again & again,
as if there were a sale on light.
And just when I can begin
to forget, to concentrate, the phone goes,
it is a whole troop of giggling
bad poems on the other end,
and they are calling, of course, Collect.

PIANO

They are bringing the piano up the hill.
From the wreck of the father's death
the piano rising.

They are bringing the piano up the hill.
In the wood the deer go down on their knees,
the kings, the queens.

They bring the piano into the house.
The keyboard is a beach where my father & I
play together again,
one hand running after the other, inseparable.

They bring the piano into the house.
Now turn, you autumn constellations, shine,
& you kings & queens of the wood
rise up, be restored.

The piano is in the house.
From the house—two-fingered, thin, beginning—
my own music rising.

The piano is in the house.

MY FATHER'S MUSIC

For fourteen years I have not heard
that Bach prelude played for me as I sat
alone in the back of the church.
Fourteen years since my dear musician died.

And she plays my father's music now,
this woman in Minnesota.
Not his, I know now,
but the sounds he served
in the dark church.   My childhood.

I thought I could write of
myself as the son rising
finally from the father, that I could be
as a rose over his grave, rooted but
staying bloomed, there at my zenith.

But now I know I must often go down, fold
over into him, & others play that music,
& weep, as today I did, hearing her,
that if I rise—and I *feel* risen—I must
go down again, & again rise,

my days a falling, a rising again,
those chords keeping me company,
those hands clustering to press & loose the music,
those forests sons walk in, seeking the father,
themselves the father, & seeking the son.

BACH'S BIRTHDAY
(Vernal Equinox, March 21, 1974)
for Mari

1

I am stuck in the First Invention.
The eleventh measure. I can't get it right,
co-ordinate the left hand and the right hand,
I play sharps for naturals, the left hand
is arthritic; it is awful.

Today is Bach's birthday.
Tonight I am taking a cherry pie
to my musical friend, who can play
Bach on organ and piano, both.
On the pie the bakery lady has squeezed
"Happy Birthday JSB" in white cream.
The lettering cost almost as much as the pie.

And I bet Mrs. Bach is busy,
baking pies for all those children
as she does every year on this day;
and tonight after supper
there will be a pie fight in paradise,
and the Bach kids will have at each other
hysterically, until they are spattered with
rhubarb, apple and cherry, pumpkin and mince,
peach and apricot, and custard of course,
and Mrs. Bach will be up half the night
running baths for—how many children was it?
(Twenty, at least!)

Today is windy, cold; but bright.
A thin snow on the streets.
You would not think our hemisphere
was leaning toward the sun again.
But it leans, all the records say so,
and my blood leans toward the sun too,
and toward Bach.

2

And here, as well as the Book of Inventions,
I have two other pages of Bach,
old, stained, torn
from my father's organ books,
too heavy to bring to America.
The first of the Eight Short Preludes and Fugues,
the one I would never tire of having him play;
I would sit in the sunlit church after mass,
the darkened church after Benediction,
and hear my father doing Bach's bidding
on the keyboards, fingering, fingering,
and doing the foot-dance with the pedals
and pushing in and pulling out stops,
busy Eddie, the musical man,
grandson of the Irish ferryman,
bringing us Bach, Bach.

The organ is called the King of Instruments.
Mari says she prefers it to the piano.
Last Sunday I heard her play it
for the first time—a time out of time—
those sounds that survive us.
Organ is like the French word "ouragan,"
meaning hurricane, and sometimes the organ
brings storms to my mind, where my father
is struggling in a small craft,
the seas tremendous.

3

Last night I fell asleep on the sofa
listening to the Matthew Passion.
Once I heard it in Helsinki,
in Holy Week, when I was twenty-one,
in a language I knew not one word of,
and felt I knew for that while
what the mystical men speak of,

that we are all one with another,
that we are each part of the other,
that all things are one.

And this morning woke,
both animals on the floor by me
as if waiting for me to wake,
and the sky lightening already,
dawn beyond the branches,
day of Bach's birth, and the earth
leaning toward the sun as if
turning over from a great dark sleep,
and the sun beginning to climb
higher and higher daily, the North warming,
the lakes losing their ice.

I lean toward the sun.
I lean toward the father.
I lean toward Bach on the hard keyboard.

Sometimes I think of myself
as a child, sometimes a giant,
and often it is the child who carries
the giant on his shoulders,
the giant weeping;
sometimes I am a young man made
of green wood, and there is
an arrow in my back, fired
by my father The Archer,
the last he loosed, and then lay back.

But now a man is climbing
the cliffs of Bach,
a man is swinging
from white rope to black rope
in the Bach gymnasium,
a man is sweating and shoveling pies
in the Bach bakery,

a man is watching over
millions of tiny clambering notes
in the Bach kindergarten,
garden of children,
Johann's millions of children buzzing
out of the Bach hives,
hot for the honey of the world.

4

And all of us trying to do
things we do not know how to,
now I am caught, now freed,
now I stop, now I begin again,
fingering, fingering; Bach's bidding.
And Mari at the instrument, daughter of men,
building those sounds
in the limitless acres of the ear,
the oaks and harvests and hurrying skies of Bach,
as the North, whose children we are, leans
toward the sun, which is climbing, leans
toward Bach, who is climbing, the ice
streaming out of his hair,
and Death, Death, *wo bist du*, where, where is your sting?

BIRD BEFORE DAWN

Bird before dawn,
bird before dawn,
I hear you

liquid in the dark,
long before
the light,

hear you
after hours of images,
tethered

to the Great Silence,
eyes closed, lips open
but no music from me;

and now though I lie
a human in a room,
I am there

in your throat,
in the wet center
where the notes swell,

without words,
with merely a man's tongue;
and O my musician,

my April chanter,
I rise, I ride
out of the winter on your song.

UNCLE FRANK

1

Frank, Frank. I stand over the lake.
Your white hair. Fall, Wisconsin; dry,
danger of fire. Hospital bed. Danger of burning.
The leaves clatter down. In England,
dead. Dry leaves rain down. Father-link.
They scrape along the ground.

2

Once, in your quiet, intent voice,
you told me
how my father and you,
a few days after your mother's death,
were standing outside the family house
and both of you felt
some person brush between you,
and both turned to see
a woman wearing a large hat
go on up and into the house
and turn to the left,
to where your parents' bedroom was.

You showed me a photo,
my father and his father, yours,
in an open car in Ireland,
turned facing the camera;
one aunt in the back; and between her
and the men in front,
the shadowy face of a woman
in a large hat.

Looking closer you could say
it was the grass and stones of the roadside
that formed her face;
but every time again I looked
I saw her among them.

3

Last June, on the train to Montana
with my brother and his wife,
I dreamed your brother Bim announced
"the death of my beloved brother Frank."
Four months later, the day
they were flying home, you were dying.
Frail friend, won't you see me here,
ever? That time in England
I showed the family films of my life here,
you could not come, your wife too ill.
On the phone you were crying.
Would you, like my father's ghost,
follow over the Atlantic the family blood
to this unlikely outpost
in the Midwest?
Would you have words for me,
to help my life, my uncle
of grass and stones? Wisconsin, Frank.
White hair, white hair. With no fear
I summon you,
at any time,
in any house I have.

4

That freezing October night
I sense the stars, loosened by frost, falling;
they splash and scatter, they soak
into the iron ground.
Once I'm woken by a cry; sweat, scared.
I think it is a child
out in the dark wood.
It must be a mouse
in an owl's claws.
Or, it is the owl itself.

In the morning, in the garden again,
I hear a sound of tearing, and turn;
a large leaf is coming down,
slower than I can believe,
so large it could have come
from no tree that grows on this land.

TALK TO ME, BABY

1

A friend at a cocktail party tells me
of being on a fishing trip up North
and meeting some men from Illinois
who showed him how to clean and filet a fish properly;
and of how, when one particular pike
was stripped almost clean, almost all of him gone,
the jaw with the razory teeth opened
and some kind of cry came from the creature,
that head on the end of almost no body;
and the man with the knife said:
"Talk to me, baby."

2

Up in the Boundary Waters last weekend
I hooked a trout, my first, and played him.
I got him to the shallows
and tried to raise him.   And the girls
got down into the water with my leather hat—
we hadn't brought a net—and I was yelling
"I've got a fish! I've got a fish!"
out into the evening, and the girls
tried to get him into the hat, and did once,
but then he was out again—a wriggle, a flap—
that fish jumped out of my hat!—
and the line, gone loose, jerked, snapped, and he was back
in the water, the hook in him.

And he didn't turn into
a glimmering girl, like he did for
young Willie Yeats,
not was he a Jesus, like for Lawrence;
he just drifted head down near the shallows,
huge, the huge hook in him.
And Louis and Phil came up in the other
canoe, and we got the flashlight on him,

and tried to get hold of him.   But then, somehow,
we lost him, drifting about, he was not there
but gone somewhere deeper into the water,
every minute darker; my hook in him.

I hooked five or six snags after that, yelling
each time that each one was a fish, bigger
than the last.   But I brought nothing living up.
And the other canoe went ghostly on the water,
silvery, like a dish with two quiet eggs in it;
and the pines were massed, dark, and stood and smelled
strong, like a bodyguard of dried fish.

3

Breathing, my brother in my house,
and breathing, his wife beside him.

Breathing, my brother in America,
his body in my bed, her body.

Their tent the color of the sun in my garden.
And they are riding West.

And both of us riding West, brother,
since we swam out of the father,

heading, six years apart,
the same way.

The dog stares at me, not knowing
why I have not fed him.
The cat crying to come in.

Whom we feed, sustain us.
Who need us, we keep breathing for.

I have seen you, at supper with friends,
put your hands to the guitar strings

and bring strong music out, seen you
sit and pick out

a tune on the piano,
on a friend's penny whistle.

To hold an instrument, to play.
To hold a pen, to write.

To do as little harm as possible
in the universe, to help

all traveling people, West, West;
you are not traveling alone,

not ever; we all go with you;
only the body stays behind.

4

When I stand on my island, a Napoleon,
one hand nailed to my chest,
the writing hand;

when I can only *stare*
at the ocean, at the birds
running and turning against the light . . .

When I am
the Illinois man and his kind,
"Talk to me, baby,"

the one with the knife inside, sometimes,
the one you may meet on your travels,
the one behind you in the line to get on the bus,

the one arranging a deal in a phone booth
as you drive past,
when I become that thing I sometimes become,

I will go into
the green of this visit, the green
you asked me to try to see

after my earlier, darker poems for you—
and this, the fourth one, darker
than I meant, since the man with the knife

swam into it—O when that killer
stands over our city, our sleeping and loving places,
tent, canoe, cabin of sweet people—

I will hear with your ears
the songs of the birds of the new world
that so quicken you, and look for

their wings that flame and flash—there! there!—
among the leaves and branches . . .

5

Too often I have wanted
to slip away, the hook in me,
to roll off the bed

and into the dark waters under it;
to drift, head down,
hide, hide, the hook in me;
to roll
in the wet ashes of the father,
wet with the death of the father,
and not try
to burn my way upward; the son, rising.

I swear to you now, I will survive,
rise up, and chant my way through these losses;

and you, you, brother, whatever that is,
same blood, you who swim

in the same waters,
you promise me to make *your* music too,
whatever the hurt;

O when we are almost only
mouth, when we are almost only a head
stuck on the pole of the body,
and the man says "Talk to me, baby,"
let's refuse him, brother, both, all of us,
and striking the spine like an instrument, inside,
like birds, with even the body broken,
our feathers fiery—there! there!—among
the leaves and branches, make
no sounds he will know;
like birds, my brother, birds of the new world, *sing*.

SUN EXERCISES

for
Chester and Carole Anderson

these flames among my friends

Note for Sun Exercises

In this poem I have tried to shed an
"unhealthy grief" which began with my
father's death in 1960, when I was 19.
Certain dreams and stories seemed to
show me a possible way to go toward
my own life.

The directions at the start of each
section come from the Hatha Yoga
exercise Soorya Namaskaram—the
Sun Salutation. The words "So Hum"
form a common mantra, intended to
quiet the mind and focus it on
the present time and place, freed
from "all other places and all
other times." "Baba Nam, Keva Lam"
is a mantra also.

The first version of this poem was
read in May 1975 at the Cathedral
Church of Saint Mark in Minneapolis;
I am very grateful to the Festival
Arts Committee of Saint Mark's, whose
commission of this poem obliged
me to tackle something I had been
circling for years.

Call me by name: the Master who dwelleth in the Vineyard,
The Boy who roameth through the town, the Young Man in the plain.
Call me by name: the Child who traveleth toward his Father,
The Child of Light who findeth his Father in the Evening.

from *Book of the Dead*
(translated by Robert Hillyer)

One: Face the Sun. Fold the hands. Legs together. Stand erect.

I am walking by the sea with my mother.

There is a jail built on the sand,
at the water's edge.
We hear faint cries from inside,
the jail rocks softly,
like a box with an animal inside it.

In a small boat my father goes by.
It is a calm sea.
Rowing with him are his father
and his father's father.
As the three men go by,
my father pauses from his rowing
and waves to us.

My sister Mary is standing on the beach.
She is staring into the sun.
Her belly swells, she must lie down.
I ask her why she lies down on the sand;
she says:
"To give birth to my pain."
After a little while, her belly subsides,
she lies quiet.

My sister Angela stands looking at the waves;
like a Queen she tries to command them:
"Go back, go back." The tide creeps forward,
licks at her feet.
Her hands are resting on a pram;
the pram is filled with fish, small fish,
of a kind you can catch in any country.

The tide comes in; she steps back,
letting the pram go:
it floats off from her.
How soon do we turn to men,
who swim in the sea?

And here is my mother, content to sit
and watch the water.
She is remembering when she was a girl,
and the long long wrinkled hair of the four sisters.
She is content to be dreaming of them
in the long afternoon.

My three women of the sand.

Peter comes up to me.
Evening already. A darker blue.
He has coils of ropes on both shoulders.
My brother is Prince of Ropes.
He says: "It's time to go."
My brother at home among heights,
which I fear.
He says: "We must rope up."

Soon we are bound together.
We walk to the base of the steep cliff.
It goes up and up,
I cannot see the top.
Evening already. A night coming down.
We make the first toe-holds,
we begin to climb
the high stone face of the father.

Two: Inhale and raise the arms. Bend backward.

You, I accuse.
You, Michael Moon.

Mad Moon Boy.
How mad you are, noboby knows.

You get drunk at dawn.
You ride the spider bareback across the dawn.

You stand on your head on the moon,
alone. Little Tomb Lover.

Ophelia, Ophelia, drifting along;
ah, such a sad song!

When you were small,
what was your nightmare?
My nightmare was
that the moon rose over the world's edge;
it stared at me; it climbed, it smiled,
and was mocking me.
If I didn't wake myself up
before it climbed too high.
I'd be dead.

What now do you dream?
I feel the shadows of Europe creep
over my sheets.
I hear the French,
I hear Agincourt and its arrows.

I see my brain,
my brain the potato,
the black three-pound potato
in an Irish field.
I hold up my brain,
caked with the dirt of ancestors,
I wave it—
do all my thoughts
come from this thing?

I rinse it in a stream
like an old washerwoman,
I race through the streets,
this moon-brain in my hands.

Eli, Eli, lama sabachtani? *

This is the night the dead headmaster
turns toward you with a fresh exam,
this is the night the crucifix clicks open
under the black gloves of the burglar.

This is the night the rat runs out
for his free gift,
this is the night the boneless bird
flies.

This is the night the children
crouch in the stone rocket,
this is the night a mother chains
her child to a dead animal.

Eddie, Eddie . . .

*My God, my God, why hast Thou forsaken me?

O you Moon,
you Potato Man,
you Toy—
how can we rid the town of this rat?

Moon, I summon you.
Michael Moon, I call you out
from your shallow grave,

from your brown bag
in the Potter's Field—come forth.
"Moon get up and mend your wounds—"
all the children know *that* song.

See, the rocking chair rocks backwards and forwards,
trying to rock itself into a man—
"Moon get up and mend your wounds—"
See, the woman croons a quiet song
to the driftwood she holds in her arms.

Moon,
Michael Moon,
mend yourself,
come forth.

Three: Exhale and bend forward till the hands are in line with the feet.
Touch the knees with your head.

Easter again.
I light a candle in the window.

On a hill in Wisconsin
I light a hundred candles,
O little prisoners,
strapped to your wicks, but dancing!

I gather dry wood from behind the house.
I pile and light it.

And I remember the Vigils, Easter Eve,
the night of the new fire;
the whole church darkened,
the priest breathing on the water of the font,
the priest taking
the huge hunk of Paschal candle
and sliding it into the water.

And the kindling of the new fire,
the passing from taper to taper
until all God's people stood
in a flickering, a silence;
each fist flowers with the new fire.

We boys went round with poles,
lifting the Lent cloths off the statues.

Now the sun sinks, into the bluffs
behind the lake.
I say to the sun: "Do you die too?"
He tells me: "No, I go down
to meet the snake, alone.
Always I return."

I rub sticks together,
I dance.
I ride the roads.
I run up and down
the hills on fire,
the peasants of Europe are marching with torches,
run run over Wisconsin now with torches,
through the abandoned farms,
roll blazing wheels down hills,
let there be
beacons on each height,
hoist fires like children
on their fathers' shoulders.

I am the Boy of New Fire.
I am the King you feast from.
I am the Fellow of Flares.

I slide down to the lake—still frozen—
I breathe my English breath three times
on this midwestern water,
and in the pool I make I dip
the moon-corpse, white as the cold
Christ-body of the father,
I the Moon Man
Easter upon myself.

There is my house on the hill, and all its lights.
If I could cut a cloth of such flame,
and all winter wear it,
if I could bless and multiply,
if I could pass out
these flames among my friends,
and every house,
like my castle of many candles,
and every family, and friend,
this night receive new fire.

Four: Inhale and move the right leg away from the body in a big backward step. Keep the hands and the left foot firmly on the ground, bending the head backward. The left knee should be between the hands.

The curtains fill with wind. April.
Blue curtains ebb and swell.

So
Hum.
I am That.
I am who I am.

And in the Book of the Dead I read
of Osiris, the dismembered King,
of Horus, his son, who must avenge him,
of Isis, her loving gathering.

I bend.
Out of the wound,
the wound's shadow.

        O
        Oooo
        Oooossss
        Oooossssiiii
        Oooossssiiiirrrr
        Oooossssiiiirrrriiii
        Oooossssiiiirrrriiiissss
        I

Children go by, to school, from school,
children in the neighborhood.

Within the King,
the King's shadow.

                    H
                    Hoooo
                    Hoooorrrr
                    Hoooorrrruuuu
                    Hoooorrrruuuussss
                    I

A little girl in a red jacket
picks up a wounded bird, with one wing gone,
and wraps him in her coat,
and takes him home.

I bend,
breathe;
out, out
of the shadow.

So
Hum.

Blue curtains swell, the dusk leaves
little shells of shadow on the sill.

I am That.
I am who I am.

"and takes him home."

Five: Inhale and hold the breath. Move the left leg from the body and, keeping both feet together and the knees off the floor, rest on the hands (arms straight) and keep the body in a straight line from head to foot.

Why do you fear the father death?
    I saw my own death. I saw my own death too.

Do you feel the father weight?
    I crawl out from under its moon.

Shall we send you back to England?
    Don't send me back to the island.

Have you done your homework?
    Everything except the algebra. I liked the geography!

Have you married a wife yet?
    I have tried to.

Do you want to look like Eddie Browne?
    I fear to become him. I long to become him.

Do you think you'd die if we sent you back to England?
    Don't send me back to the island.

Are birds old enough for you?
    Yes! Yes!

Does the trees' green please you?
    New, ancient, they please me in my deep heart.

Are you mad sometimes?
    Ball and chain. Ball and chain.

Do you fear yourself sometimes?
    Sometimes I fear myself.

What is music to you?
    It is my marrow.

What are words then?
    Words are my bones, with their marrow of music.

What is your brain to you?
    My brain is a potato. I have said it already.

Are you afraid of your brain sometimes?
    Afraid of my brain.

Why Browne with an 'e'?
    Others before me . . . I had no control . . .

Where is your brain from?
    Mostly from Ireland. From England also.

Are you able to love someone?
    Yes . . . No . . . Sometimes . . . There have been criticisms . . .

Have you got something in your mouth?
    No.

Are you still afraid of the headmaster?
    Still afraid of him.

Do you still smell the funny smells of the priests?
    I smell them.

Is the sun rising?
    I see him! I see him! Soon!

What about this matter of the moon?
    I am trying to cope.

Do you bend your body?
    I do.

Will you take this body for what it is?
    I will.

Do you accept this death you will have?
    I try to.

Do you promise yourself?
    I promise myself. I have made promises to others also.

Are you the Moon Man?
    No more . . . Sometimes . . . No more.

Is all this difficult for you?
    Yes.

Six: Exhale and lower the body to the floor. In this position,
only eight portions of the body come in contact with the floor.
The abdominal region is raised and, if possible, the nose is also kept off
the floor, the forehead only touching it.

two feet
two knees
two nipples
two eyes

breathe out
breathe out
all the old hours
here you are on the ground

       I am alone in the Black Forest
       my bicycle is broken
       my friends leave me

the idea is to loosen
your stiff center
the idea is to earn
the quiet heart you can have

       I am balanced on the handlebars
       he is bicycling to Mass
       mist   chestnuts

two feet
two knees
two nipples
two eyes

the abdominal region
is raised
if possible the nose
is also kept off the floor

I am sitting by his bed
a child cries all night
from the children's ward
all night a pipe drips
outside the waiting room

the idea is to peel off
all exterior music
the idea is to drink
the cup that is passed to you

I am sitting by his bed
a doctor, a nurse, come by—
"Who are you?" I say
(all mornings, mornings shall I say it)
"This gentleman is my father"

two feet
two knees
two nipples
two eyes

I am lying face down on the earth
eyes closed, I stare down
I smell the April in the earth
I am lying on all the flowers

the idea is to mend
the idea is to gather
the separated parts
to achieve the quiet heart

I am lying down on the flowers
I am learning to swim on them
I am a child
I am a man
I am who I am

two feet
two knees
two nipples
two eyes

                    I am lying on all the flowers
                    Some men in a boat going by
                    I am learning to swim
                    He watching me
                    He watching among the flowers

So

                    I breathe

Hum

                    I swim

I am a man

I am That

I am who I am

*Seven: Inhale and bend backward as much as possible, bending
the spine to the maximum.*

A friend, a student, calls me,
who has dreamed of me;
that I have fallen,
opened an old wound
in the back of my head.

Another calls,
that I was walking with them in a field,
that I fell down a black hole
and was smothering.

In my own sleep I visit a vineyard,
where a man and a woman in work aprons
tell me they are growing
a mandala for me. It is my own.
Soon they can take me to see it.

Sometimes I sense an ocean near my door.
Sometimes my dog looks at me,
as if there were something he would say . . .

On my shelf, a piece of driftwood from Maine,
from a woman named Margaret.
She has inked these characters on it—
sun   rain   and then   mysterious light

I love my house.
I love my house that will not endure.

I climb to the roof and look out over the city.
I break the bread of the dawn.

Geese have passed over, fresh from the South;
I feel their flight.

I would bless my friends, near, far,
in their houses where they are sleeping;

in their sun,
in their rain,
in their mysterious light.

*Eight: Exhale and lift the body. Keep the feet and heels flat on
the floor.*

He tells his sister to dance.
She who is in pain.

Your pain is my pain too.
Our task, to move to the madness.

He tells his sister to dance.

Mary, you have seen
those trees near the sea, bent backward,
old, old, bent by those winds.

You, who were a dancer, I tell you,
now dance again, dance always,
even if it is
your pain that moves you.

I too tried
to stand against my pain.

But now in storms I flutter,
not distinct from them,
like smoke among its flames,
not separate, not separate!

You who once rushed and uprooted
roses from your garden
when I was leaving our country,
you who once poured
roses into my arms,

here now in America, ten years gone,
see now, I dance with you!

Pain loves to find
a thing rooted, that will not move.

I hear a sound
outside my life, it is you
as you start to move your branches—

Mary! Mary! I am dancing with you
over an ocean,

in my house on the hill,
in my own rooms and storms.

Christ was not stiff on his tree,
like a fish he rippled out
from under the nails!

Happier, happier are we not
both now?
O painful, painful we people are,
but once again dancing!

Nine: Inhale and bring the right foot along the level of the hands:
left foot and knee should touch the ground. Look up, bending the spine
slightly, as in number four.

In my dream, I was weeping.
Then you, my father, were there,
in the same room.

I remember the time
my aunt came into the room
and told you your father was dead.
I hardly knew anyone then who had died.
I remember the way
you put your head into your hands.

In my dream. I was going on a journey.
I had a pack on my back. I was weeping.
You said: "Don't cry. Take this knife.
You will need it on your journey."

With the knife you gave me I made
my story of the Sun Fetcher—

the world is dark, without dawn,
the sun will not rise.
The moon rules the sky, moon, moon.
whitening, withering the crops.
The boy is sent out to find,
to fetch the sun.

I carved the story—

he battles with the black dog,
the white thorn strapped to his head,
he battles the moon, the north wind;
he comes at last
over the world's edge to find
the sun caught in the branches
of the great tree;
and trapped in the tree's roots,
the father.

Now all birds
come, to help him
pull apart the branches;
and now the sun again sails up,
the roots give up the father.
Man and boy together go home
through the warming world.

I remember how we'd go
to light candles in churches,
to pray for the souls
of the Faithful Departed.

You said: Never forget them,
when you are a man.
Fetch them back, into your life,
again and again.

Eddie. Eddie Departed.
With the knife you give me.
The story, the story for the journey
I in my turn am on.

Ten: Exhale and bring the left leg forward. Keep the knees straight and bring the head down to the knees as in the third position.

Baba Nam   Keva Lam
Father Name   Everything Name
He comes

In a north field I stand
in the dark before dawn
I am Horus
I am Osiris
I am the Prince of the Field

He comes

The field is primitive
The leaves shake
I shake with the primitive fear

I feel weapons I cannot see
I feel the grinding of tools
of the old tribes
I feel a fur on me

Baba Nam   Keva Lam
Father Name   Everything Name
He comes

I stand in Minnesota, in my North
in Egypt I stand
I stand with friends in a threshing field in Spain
with Roy, with Eve, under the olive trees
with Tim on a rock in Finland, facing Russia
by Lake Superior, with Peter

The trees are seething
they seethe with the early fear
I thirst for the quiet heart

Baba Nam   Keva Lam
Father Name   Everything Name
He comes

Now, like a castle that swells its walls
now, now, my Lord

And the trees' tops
tipped with the new fire

Now, the Sun Boat
now, in the smell of the blood of birth
now, now, my Lord

The old skin splits, drops
in a heap at my feet,
now the ancient skin, the shadow,
scuttles away

Now, coming
now, from the tomb
now, now, my Lord

Is it you?
You who went down
to do your battle alone?
You said to me:
"Always I return."

The trees steeped
in their fresh fire

I lift my branches
I let fall
my huge head
down, down
I bend

I stir the earth with my hair
like a river
I breathe—

how many mornings—
all my life shall I greet thee—

my lost returned
my Life Giver

Thou, my risen Lord
Thy light on me

Eleven: Raise the arms over head and bend backward inhaling, as in
position number two.

It is May again; my month.
The month of Mary, whom my father loved.

In my green time, I feel a child again.
I touch the hem of the robe of the huge May.

I feed my birds, and I hear them—
grosbeak, nuthatch, goldfinch, chickadee—

and you, red cardinal among the leaves,
is it me you are calling?

You are too fat,
you bend the twig you sit on!

The dog wants in, the cat wants out.
I move the sick plant into the sun,
myself I move.
I feel a wind; I see the trees lift;
I open all my doors, I hear
the mourning dove, as in
so many boyhood mornings, the same song.

Sometimes I feel an ocean near my door.
A mother is sitting, watching the water,
her children are playing in the waves.
One boy stands and watches
some men in a boat going by.

A rain comes: O like a cracked dry
    cooking pot I am,
        that this rain freshens and fills,

O mending now, now the Green Man
    I am in my suit of leaves,
        now walk

among things I more and more touch,
    more and more bless,
        my days, my hours

on the earth—
    I am who I am—my father's son—
        in these positions of praise.

Twelve: Exhale. Drop the arms. Relax.

May 1975
Minneapolis

Carnegie-Mellon Poetry

Books in the Carnegie-Mellon University Press Poetry
Series are distributed by the University of Pittsburgh Press,
127 N. Bellefield Avenue, Pittsburgh Pennsylvania 15260.